THE SCIENCE BEHIND

Growth

Chris Oxlade

Chicago, Illinois

www.capstonepub.com
Visit our website to find out more information about Heinemann-Raintree books.

To order:

☎ Phone 888-454-2279

💻 Visit www.capstonepub.com to browse our catalog and order online.

Edited by Claire Throp, Megan Cotugno, and Vaarunika Dharmapala
Designed by Steve Mead
Original illustrations © Capstone Global Library Ltd 2012
Illustrations by Oxford Designers & Illustrators
Picture research by Ruth Blair

Originated by Capstone Global Library Ltd
Printed and bound in China by Leo Paper Products Ltd

15 14 13 12 11
10 9 8 7 6 5 4 3 2 1

Library of Congress Cataloging-in-Publication Data
Oxlade, Chris.
  Growth / Chris Oxlade.
    p. cm.—(The science behind)
  Includes bibliographical references and index.
  ISBN 978-1-4109-4490-0 (hc)—ISBN 978-1-4109-4501-3 (pb) 1. Growth—Juvenile literature. 2. Life cycles (Biology)—Juvenile literature. I. Title.
  QH511.O95 2012
    571.8'1—dc23   2011014634

Acknowledgments
We would like to thank the following for permission to reproduce photographs: Corbis pp. **14** (© Ralph A. Clevenger), **16** (© Dennis Kunkel Microscopy, Inc./Visuals Unlimited); Photolibrary p. **10** (Juniors Bildarchiv); Shutterstock pp. **7** (© Hannamariah), **8** (© Gelpi), **9** (© Zurijeta), **11** (© AnetaPics), **13** (© Gayvoronskaya_yana), **18** (© oneo), **19** (© Valua Vitaly), **20** (© Morgan Lane Photography), **21** (© Dmitriy Shironosov), **22** (© Philip Lange), **25** (© YanLev).

Cover photograph reproduced with permission of Corbis (© Keren Su).

We would like to thank Nancy Harris for her invaluable help in the preparation of this book.

Every effort has been made to contact copyright holders of any material reproduced in this book. Any omissions will be rectified in subsequent printings if notice is given to the publisher.

All the Internet addresses (URLs) given in this book were valid at the time of going to press. However, due to the dynamic nature of the Internet, some addresses may have changed, or sites may have changed or ceased to exist since publication. While the author and publisher regret any inconvenience this may cause readers, no responsibility for any such changes can be accepted by either the author or the publisher.

Contents

Look for these boxes:

Stay safe
These boxes tell you how to keep yourself and your friends safe from harm.

In your day
These boxes show you how science is a part of your daily life.

Measure up!
These boxes give you some fun facts and figures to think about.

Some words appear in bold, **like this**. You can find out what they mean by looking at the green bar at the bottom of the page or in the glossary.

What Is Growth?

Have you measured your height recently? Have you grown taller? Have you lost your baby teeth yet? Your arms are probably getting longer, and your hands are getting bigger. Perhaps you have just bought new shoes because your feet are bigger.

These changes are all clues that you are growing. **Growth** is the name that scientists give to these changes. As you grow, you also learn skills such as walking and talking.

Here you can see how a small child grows into an adult.

1 year

5 years

growth   process of getting bigger

Your life cycle

Growth is a natural process. It is part of your life cycle. A life cycle is how an animal is born, grows, has young of its own, and eventually dies.

In your day

The next time you go to school, look at the other children on the playground. How can you tell that some children are older than you? How can you tell that some children are younger than you? What are the clues?

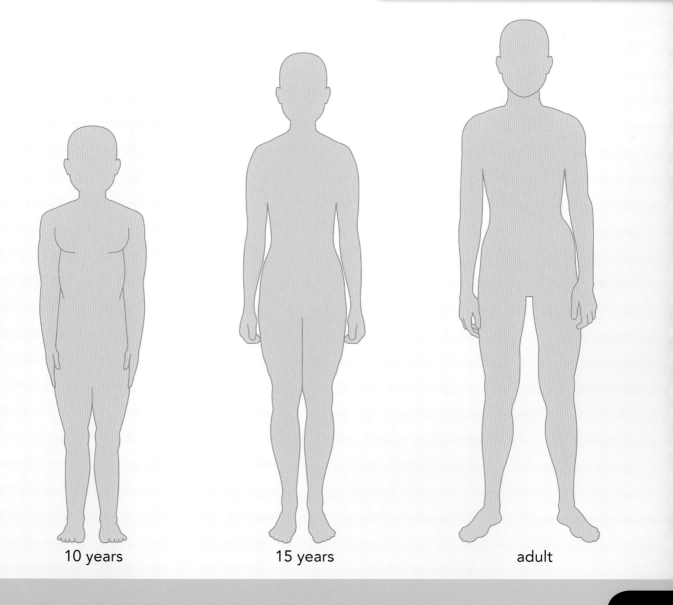

10 years   15 years   adult

How Do We Grow?

Have you seen photographs of yourself when you were a few days or weeks old? Then you were a tiny baby. You had just been born, but you had been growing for nine months inside your mother before that.

You grew from a tiny group of **cells** called an **embryo**, which was smaller than the period at the end of this sentence. The tiny group of cells grew larger and larger. After a few weeks, it began to look like a tiny human. It had tiny arms and legs, a head, and a **heart** that was beating. It was still only the size of a jellybean.

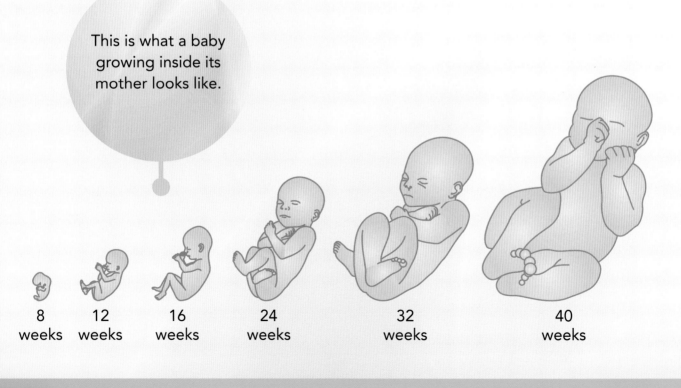

This is what a baby growing inside its mother looks like.

| 8 weeks | 12 weeks | 16 weeks | 24 weeks | 32 weeks | 40 weeks |

cell   smallest part of a living thing
embryo   tiny ball of cells that grows into an animal

Finally, after nine months of growing, you were born. You were a tiny copy of your parents.

Newborn babies sleep most of the time.

Stay safe

Young babies are very interested in the things around them. They often pick things up and put them in their mouths. They can choke on small objects, so it is important not to let them have small toys.

Baby to adult

After a baby is born, it continues growing. Its bones grow longer and thicker. At first, a baby's bones are quite soft. Even a baby's skull is soft. The bones get harder and stronger as they grow. The baby's **muscles** grow larger and stronger, too. All its **organs**, such as its heart, **lungs**, and **stomach**, also keep growing.

New skills

A baby learns new skills. After a few months, it learns to roll over. Then it learns to sit up and crawl. It learns to use its hands to feed itself. After about a year, it learns to walk. Then it slowly learns to talk.

When a baby is a few months old, it learns to push itself up and start to crawl.

muscle   part of your body that makes your skeleton bend and move
organ   part of your body that does a job, such as your heart or lungs

Humans keep growing for about 20 years. By the time they have stopped getting bigger, they are adults.

At about six years old, a child's baby teeth begin to be replaced with adult teeth.

Measure up!

How often do you need new shoes? It might be three or four times each year. That is because your feet get longer and wider as you grow. What size are your shoes? Look in some shoes you have outgrown to see what size you used to be.

lung   part of your body where air goes when you breathe
stomach   part of an animal's body where food is broken up

More Life Cycles

Does your family have a pet cat, dog, or rabbit? These animals grow in the same way as humans. They have a similar life cycle. That is because they are all **mammals**, like humans.

A puppy grows inside its mother's body, just like a human baby. It is born after growing for about nine weeks. Puppies slowly learn skills such as staying clean and hunting. After a year or two, they have grown into adult dogs and can have their own puppies.

Puppies learn skills for hunting and defending themselves by play fighting.

mammal   kind of animal, such as a human, dog, or cat

Kangaroo babies

When a kangaroo baby, called a "joey," is born, it looks like a jellybean. It is about the size of your little finger. It cannot see and it has no hair. It stays in a pocket on its mother's belly, called a pouch, until it has grown big enough to take care of itself.

Stay safe

Many animals take care of their babies until the babies are big enough to take care of themselves. Your parents take care of you. They will feed you and make sure you are safe until you can take care of yourself.

This joey is staying safe inside its mother's pouch. As a joey grows bigger, it begins to spend more and more time outside the pouch.

pouch

Growing in eggs

Have you ever seen birds' eggs in a nest? Or have you found pieces of shell from a bird's egg? After a female bird has laid an egg, a baby bird, called a chick, grows inside the egg. When a chick is fully grown, it breaks out through the egg's shell. This is called **hatching**. The chick's parents feed it until it is ready to live on its own.

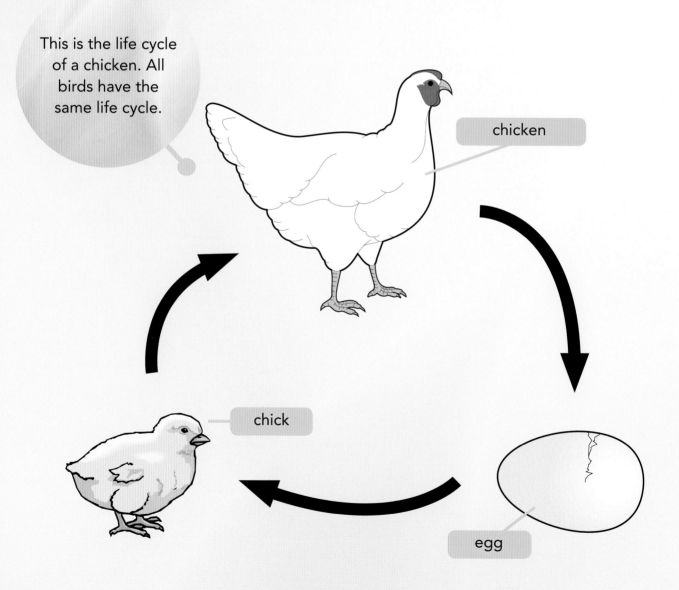

This is the life cycle of a chicken. All birds have the same life cycle.

chicken

chick

egg

hatch   when a chick breaks out of its egg

Reptiles' eggs

Animals called **reptiles** also lay eggs. Snakes, lizards, and crocodiles are reptiles. Their eggs have a shell that feels like leather. When the eggs hatch, most young reptiles take care of themselves. Their parents do not need to take care of them.

Birds and reptiles have a different life cycle than humans and most other mammals.

white

shell

yolk

You can see the different parts of an egg when you break one for cooking.

In your day

An egg's shell protects the growing chick. The clear part, called the white, also protects the chick. The yellow part is the yolk. The yolk is food for the growing chick. Take a look inside an egg the next time you help to bake a cake or cookies.

reptile   kind of animal, such as a lizard or snake

Changing Shape

You have probably watched **caterpillars** and butterflies in the park or in your backyard. Caterpillars and butterflies have very different shapes. Did you know that a caterpillar can be a baby butterfly?

Here you can see a caterpillar (left), its hard shell (center), and a butterfly (right).

When a butterfly's egg **hatches**, a caterpillar crawls out. It eats lots of leaves and grows very quickly. After a few weeks, it stops eating. It fixes itself to a leaf and grows a hard shell. Then it slowly changes into a butterfly.

caterpillar   long, crawling creature that can change into a butterfly

Growing and changing

Frogs also change shape as they grow into adults. **Tadpoles** hatch from frogs' eggs. A tadpole slowly changes shape into a frog as it grows. This change takes a few weeks. When an animal changes shape the way a butterfly or frog does, the change is called **metamorphosis**.

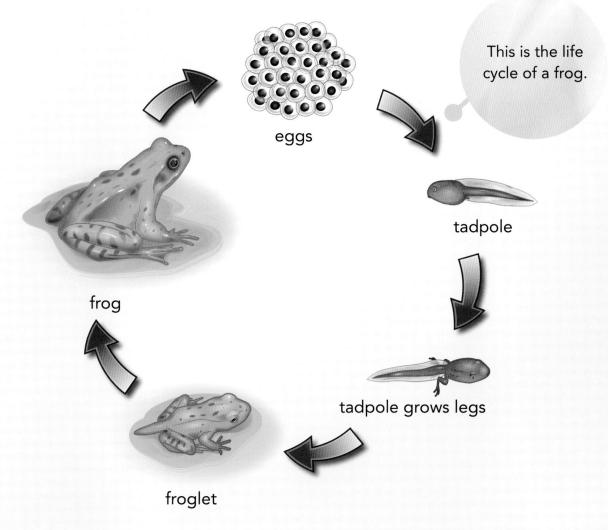

This is the life cycle of a frog.

eggs

tadpole

tadpole grows legs

froglet

frog

---

tadpole baby frog that is small and black and looks like a tiny fish
metamorphosis when an animal changes shape as it grows

Growing Cells

Take a look at your arm. What do you think it is made from? There is skin on the outside, and blood, **muscles**, and **nerves** are on the inside. All these parts are made of tiny **cells**. Skin is made of skin cells. Muscles are made of muscle cells. Blood contains blood cells, and nerves are made of nerve cells.

This is what red blood cells look like through a microscope. They are so small that you could not see them without one.

nerve   cell that sends messages to and from the brain

Making more cells

All animals are made from different sorts of cells. Animals grow by making more cells. To make a new cell, a cell splits in two. Most animals start as a single cell. Then the cell splits up to make two. Then these two split up to make four. Slowly, the cells split up to make the trillions of cells in an animal's body. This is called cell division.

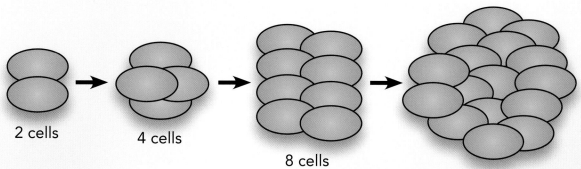

2 cells

4 cells

8 cells

16 cells

This is how two cells split up to make many more cells.

Measure up!

Skin cells are always falling off! Each day you lose about 50 million of them. That is about 0.04 of an ounce (1 gram) of skin each day. Don't worry, though, because new skin cells are always growing to replace them.

Healthy Growth

Your body cannot grow without help. You need to give it the right **nutrients** to make it grow. That means you have to eat the right kinds of food. For example, your teeth and bones need a nutrient called calcium to grow properly. You get calcium from milk.

This mother pig is feeding her piglets milk.

Eating the right food

Eating the right things starts as soon as an animal is born or **hatches**. **Mammals** such as humans, dogs, and cats drink their mothers' milk for the first few weeks or months of their lives. The milk contains all the nutrients that the baby mammal needs to grow. Baby animals that grow in eggs, such as birds, snakes, and frogs, get the food they need from inside their eggs.

nutrient   material in food that your body needs to grow and live

After a few months, human babies start eating solid foods such as fruits and vegetables. The food contains all the nutrients a baby needs to keep growing.

This baby is a few months old and is learning to eat solid food.

In your day

Have you ever looked at the information on packages of food? It tells you about the food inside. Take a closer look at the information. See if you can find out how much calcium you get from milk with your favorite breakfast cereal.

Kinds of nutrients

Rice, pasta, and bread all contain nutrients called carbohydrates. Carbohydrates give your body the **energy** it needs to work. Your body also gets energy from nutrients called fats. Fats are important, but you should not eat too many of them. They come from foods such as nuts, meat, and cheese.

pasta contains carbohydrates

vegetables contain minerals

cheese contains fats and proteins

fruits contain vitamins

You need nutrients called proteins to make and repair your body. Proteins come from meat, fish, eggs, milk, and cheese. Your body also needs nutrients called vitamins and minerals, which you can get from fruits and vegetables.

energy something we get from food that allows us to do work, such as running

A balanced diet

You have to eat a mixture of different foods to get all the things you need to grow healthily. This is called a balanced diet. Your meals should contain pasta, rice or potatoes, vegetables, proteins, **dairy products**, and fruits.

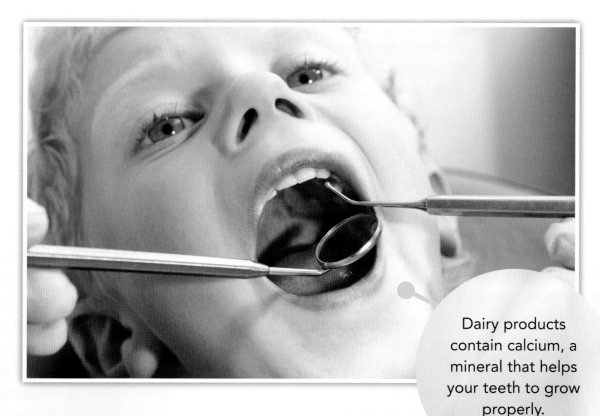

Dairy products contain calcium, a mineral that helps your teeth to grow properly.

Stay safe

When did you last go to the dentist? You might see a doctor if you are feeling sick, and the doctor helps to make you better. You should also go to the dentist regularly to make sure your teeth are healthy.

dairy product   milk, or food made from milk, such as butter, cheese, and yogurt

Always Growing

Every few weeks you have to cut your fingernails to stop them from getting too long. Fingernails grow fast, and they will keep growing even when you are an adult. Your toenails keep growing, too. So does your hair.

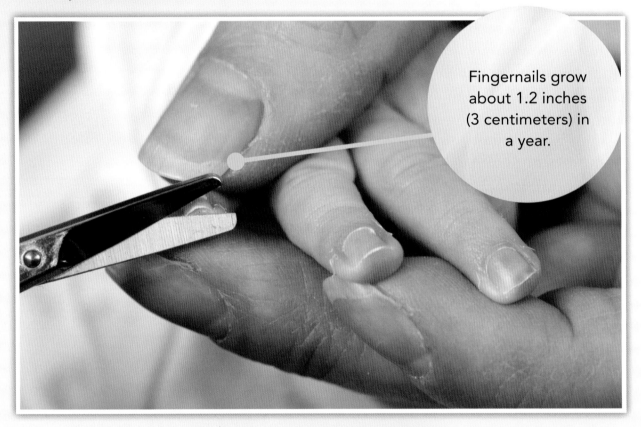

Fingernails grow about 1.2 inches (3 centimeters) in a year.

Some parts of other animals keep growing, too, such as a dog's claws and a rabbit's teeth. A dog's claws grow because they wear away as the dog walks. A rabbit's teeth grow because they wear down as the rabbit eats.

Repairing and replacing

Inside your body, **cells** are dying all the time. You lose billions of skin cells and blood cells every day. Millions of new cells grow to replace them. Some animals can even grow new legs and tails if they lose them. Newts and salamanders can do this.

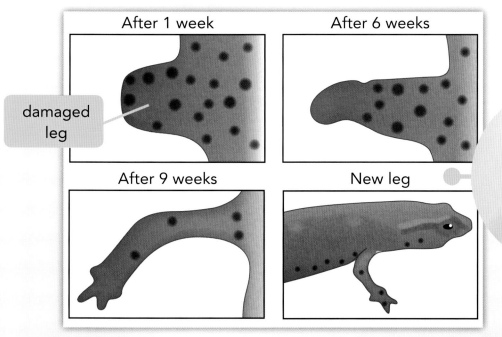

After 1 week

After 6 weeks

damaged leg

After 9 weeks

New leg

Here you can see how long it takes for a salamander to grow a new leg.

In your day

What happens when you bruise or scratch yourself? A bruise or scratch means your skin is damaged. After a few days, the bruise or scratch disappears. New cells have grown to repair the damage.

Science in Your Life

Did you realize that so much science was going on in your body as you grow?

Science explains all sorts of things that happen during **growth**. It explains what happens as a baby grows inside its mother. It explains how humans grow from babies to adults, as well as the changes that happen as they grow. Science also explains the changes that happen to other animals as they grow.

Science explains why you need to eat a healthy, balanced diet. This diet includes a mixture of different types of food, such as bread, meat, milk, fruits, and vegetables.

In your day

Try to remember all the science you have learned about growth in this book. Think about how you are growing and how the babies, children, and animals you see each day are growing.

The end of life

Animals do not live forever. Some animals die a few days after they stop growing. Other animals live for many years after they stop growing. Animals usually die because their bodies wear out and cannot repair themselves anymore.

If you take care of your body, you will grow into a healthy adult.

Try It Yourself

Measure your height and weight

Parents, nurses, and doctors check babies and children to make sure they are growing properly. They normally measure height and weight. Try the activity below to measure yourself, your family, and your friends.

What you need:

- tape measure
- scale
- large book
- pencil and paper

What to do:

1. Stand against a wall and hold the book on top of your head. Use the tape measure to measure from the floor to the bottom edge of the book.

2. Write down your name, your age, and your height (in feet and inches).

3. Weigh yourself on a scale. Write down your weight in pounds next to your height.

4. Repeat steps 1 and 2 with your brothers and sisters or friends. Write down their names, ages, heights, and weights, too.

5. Compare your results. Are older children taller than you? Do they weigh more? Are girls or boys taller?

Name	Age	Height (feet, inches)	Weight (pounds)
Amina	8	4 feet, 0 inches	46
Tom	8	4 feet, 1 inch	53
Katie	10	4 feet, 7 inches	71
Chen	12	4 feet, 11 inches	88

Glossary

caterpillar long, crawling creature that can change into a butterfly

cell smallest part of a living thing. A cell is like a building block for making animals and plants.

dairy product milk, or food made from milk, such as butter, cheese, and yogurt

embryo tiny ball of cells that grows into an animal

energy something we get from food that allows us to do work, such as running

growth process of getting bigger

hatch when a chick breaks out of its egg

heart part that pumps blood around an animal's body

lung part of your body where air goes when you breathe

mammal kind of animal, such as a human, dog, or cat

metamorphosis when an animal changes shape as it grows

muscle part of your body that makes your skeleton bend and move

nerve cell that sends messages to and from the brain

nutrient material in food that your body needs to grow and live

organ part of your body that does a job, such as your heart or lungs

reptile kind of animal, such as a lizard or snake

stomach part of an animal's body where food is broken up

tadpole baby frog that is small and black and looks like a tiny fish

Find Out More

Use these resources to find more fun and useful information about the science behind growth.

Books

Ballard, Carol. *Bones* (*Body Focus*). Chicago: Heinemann Library, 2009.

Parker, Steve. *How Do My Muscles Get Strong?* (*Inside My Body*). Chicago: Raintree, 2011.

Royston, Angela. *Butterfly (Life Cycle of a...)*. Chicago: Heinemann Library, 2009.

Royston, Angela. *Chicken (Life Cycle of a...)*. Chicago: Heinemann Library, 2009.

Royston, Angela. *Frog (Life Cycle of a...)*. Chicago: Heinemann Library, 2009.

Royston, Angela. *Kangaroo (Life Cycle of a...)*. Chicago: Heinemann Library, 2009.

Websites

www.choosemyplate.gov/foodgroups/index.html
Learn about the different food groups and how to eat a healthy, balanced diet at this website.

http://teams.lacoe.edu/documentation/classrooms/ judi/life/activities/cycles/life_cycles.html
Try some of the great activities on this website and test your knowledge about life cycles. Which comes first, the tadpole or the eggs?

http://kidshealth.org/kid/htbw/bones.html#cat119
Learn all about bones, including how bones grow and develop, at this website.

http://kidshealth.org/kid/stay_healthy/food/fitness_ nutrition_center.html#cat119
At this website you can learn how to help your body grow strong and healthy.

Index